Bernardino Luini, *Bust of Christ*

Jesus

IMAGES OF CHRIST IN ART

Selections from
The King James Version of the Bible

Edited by Marion Wheeler

BCL PRESS • NEW YORK

© 1988 O.G. Publishing Corp.
Text ©1988 Marion Michael Wheeler
Compilation © 1988 Chameleon Books, Inc.

This edition published by BCL Press/Book Creation, LLC, New York,
by arrangement with O.G. Publishing Corp.
Previously published as: His Face: Images of Christ in Art

Produced by
Chameleon Books, Inc.
31 Smith Road
Chesterfield, MA 01012

Designer, Picture Editor: Arnold Skolnick

ISBN 1-932302-05-0

Printed in China

CONTENTS

*H*istorically, Jesus Christ's physical appearance remains a mystery. No one knows what he actually looked like. Nowhere in the gospels is he described, and no likeness of him of any kind in any form can be dated conclusively to the years of his life on earth. Yet his face is the most familiar and recognizable in Western iconography.

For centuries, rendering the essential qualities of Christ's divinity and humanity has dominated the creative energies and imaginations of the world's artists—from early unknown painters to the most celebrated masters. And, although each artist's conception is an individual representation of Christ, and each image may differ in terms of specific physical characteristics, the image portrayed is always immediately identifiable as that of Christ. For, although he is represented as a man among men, women, and children, the face of Christ, as rendered by the great painters, always reflects the unique dual nature of Christ as God and man. The result of this considerable artistic achievement is a legacy of visions of Jesus Christ that is at once aesthetically magnificent and spiritually enriching.

The idea for this book came after visiting the great art collections in America and Europe. So many of the faces of Christ remained vivid in our minds long after the memory of the paintings in which they appear had faded. Who could forget the gravely triumphant image of the resurrected Christ as painted by Piero della Francesca? Or Paolo Veronese's compassionate yet sorrowful Christ carrying the cross? Or Raphael's innocent yet preternaturally wise infant Jesus? The power of these images remains long after they are first seen and is renewed each time they are seen again, even in reproductions.

The choice of images in this book is necessarily arbitrary. It does not attempt to be anything other than a representative selection from the thousands of depictions of Jesus Christ in art. Those selected date from the twelfth century through the twentieth. Italian, Spanish, French, German, Dutch, and Flemish artists predominate simply because they produced so many of the most spiritually compelling and inspiring portraits of Christ.

Grateful acknowledgment is made to all those who helped produce this book; special thanks are owed to John Roberts and Joel Rosenman, Astrid Seeburg, Alan Kanterman, Joseph Lada, Roberta Halpern, Marilee Talman, Stephen Frankel, and Perry Brooks for their invaluable assistance.

M. W.

HIS YOUTH

Behold, a virgin shall be with child, and shall bring forth a son, and they shall call his name Emmanuel, which being interpreted is, God with us.

— MATTHEW 1:23

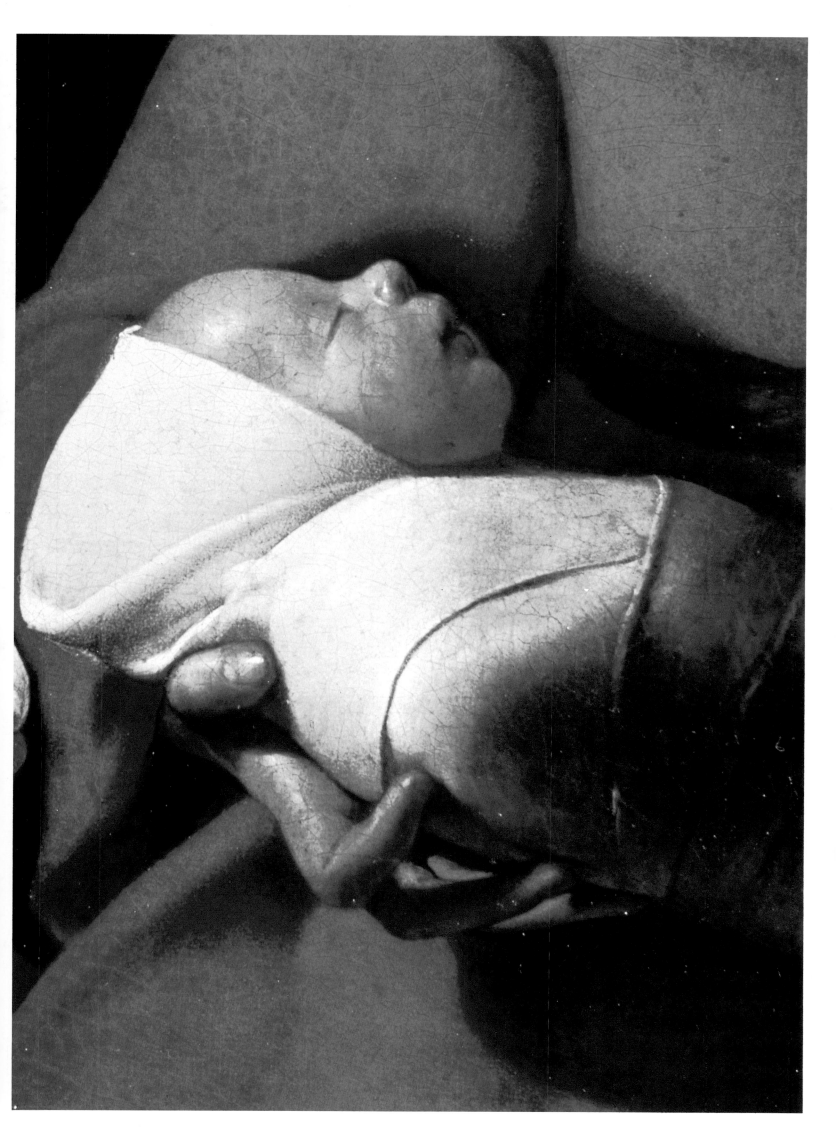

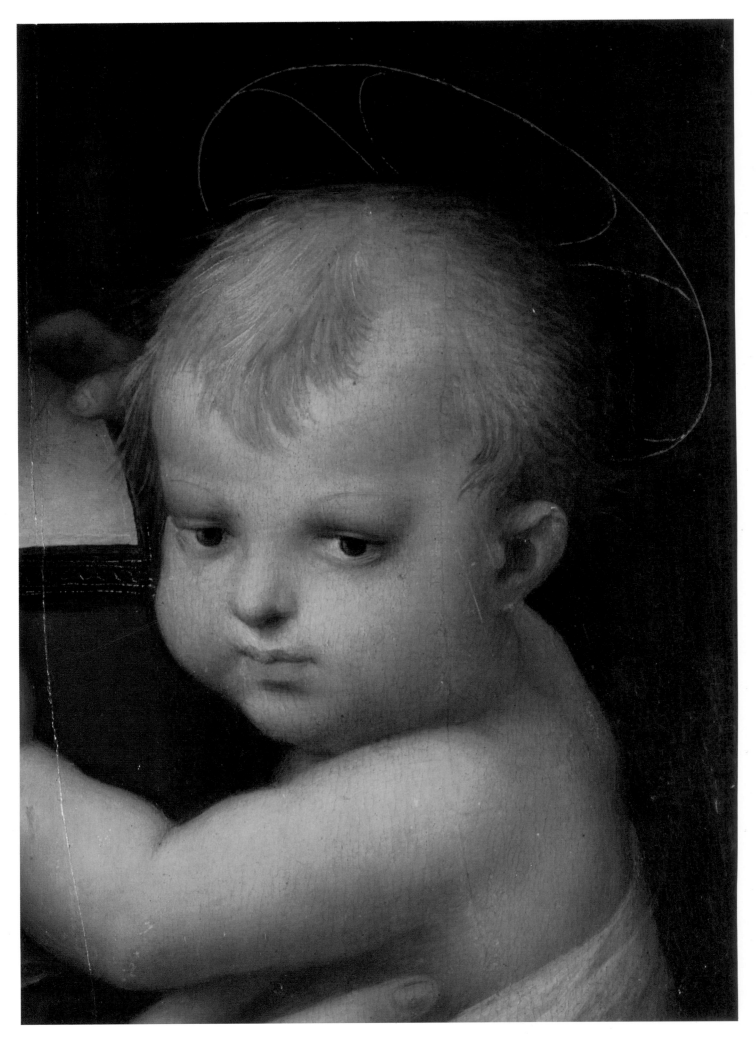

Raphael, *Madonna of the Grand Duke*

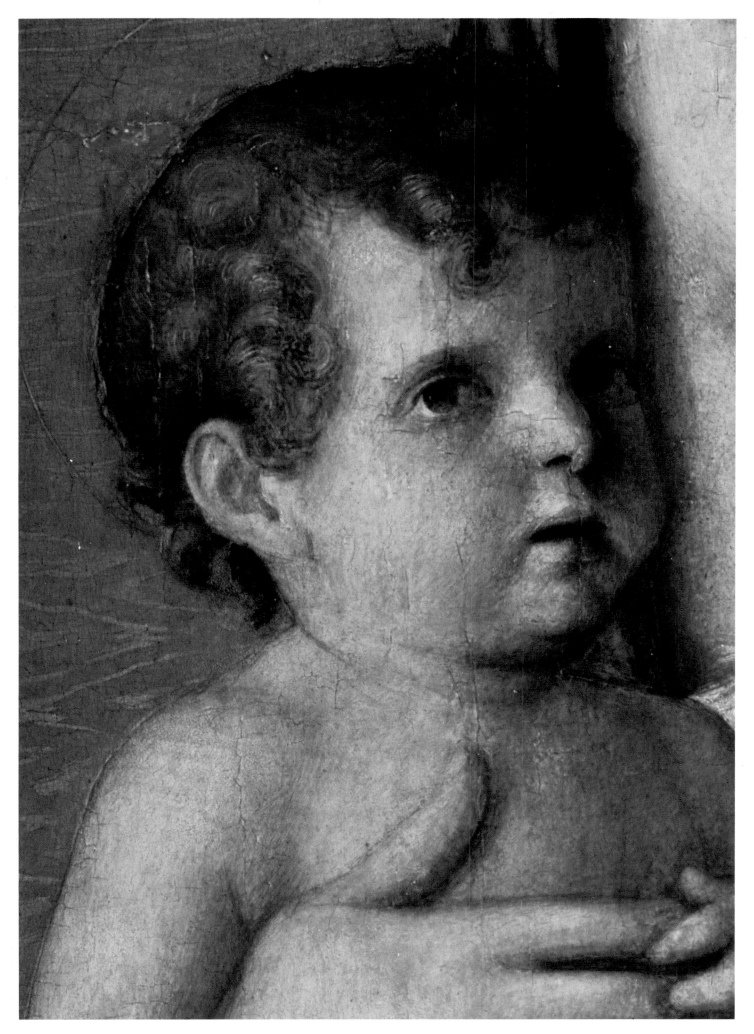

Giovanni Bellini, *Madonna degli Alberelli*

Neroccio de' Landi, *Madonna and Child with St. Anthony Abbot and St. Sigismund*

The School of Piero della Francesca, *Virgin and Child with Angels*

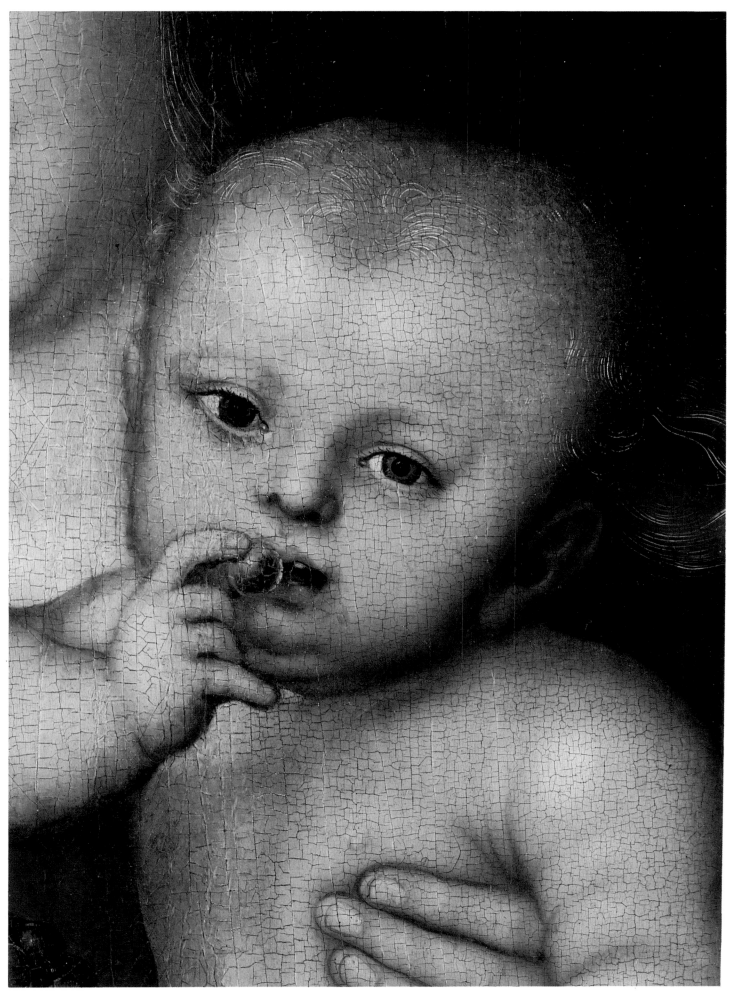

above: Lucas Cranach (the Elder), *Madonna and Child*

opposite: Domenico Ghirlandaio, *Madonna and Child*

above: Raphael, *The Alba Madonna*

opposite: Giovanni Battista Tiepolo, *Madonna of the Goldfinch*

above: Ludovico Carracci, *The Dream of St. Catherine of Alexandria*

opposite: Michelangelo Merisi da Caravaggio, *Madonna dei Palafrenieri*

Jacopo da Pontormo, *The Holy Family*

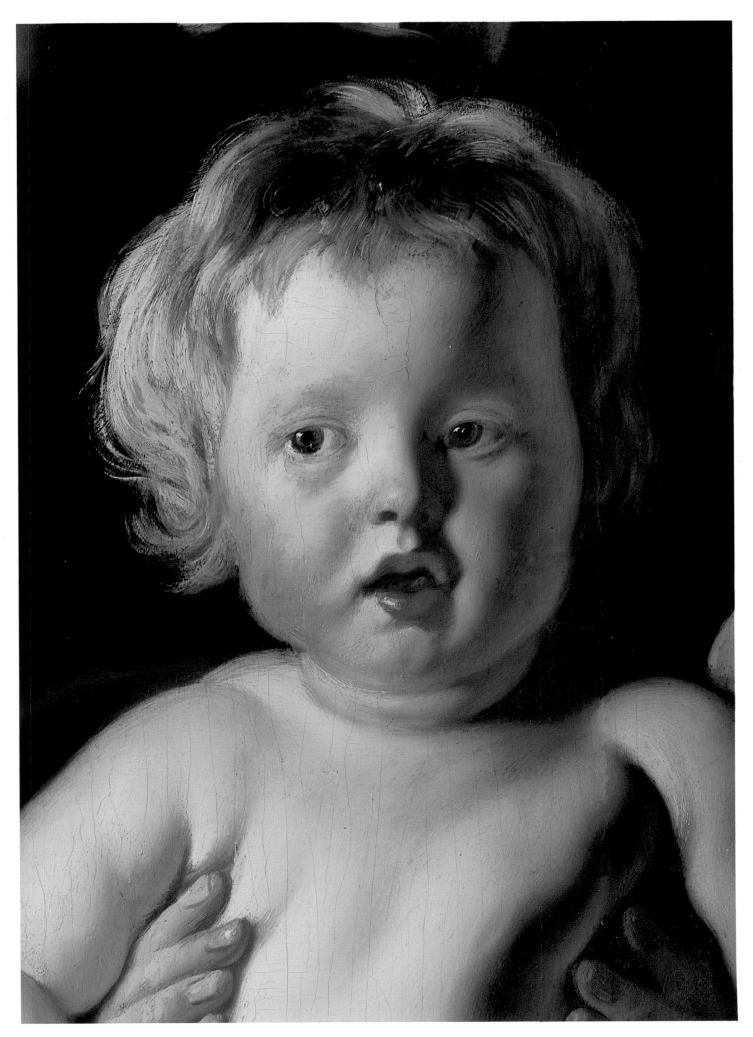

Jacob Jordaens, *The Holy Family and St. John the Baptist*

Byzantine (13th century), *Madonna and Child on a Curved Throne*

Margaritone d'Arezzo, *Madonna and Child Enthroned*

And the child grew, and waxed strong in spirit, filled with wisdom: and the grace of God was upon him.

– LUKE 2:40

Georges de La Tour, *St. Joseph the Carpenter*

*And when he was twelve years old, they went up to
Jerusalem after the custom of the feast. And when they
had fulfilled the days, as they returned, the child Jesus
tarried behind in Jerusalem; and Joseph and his mother
knew not of it.*

– LUKE 2:42–43

*And it came to pass, that after three days they found him
in the temple, sitting in the midst of the doctors, both hearing
them, and asking them questions. And all that heard him were
astonished at his understanding and his answers.*

– LUKE 2:46–47

Master of the Catholic Kings, *Christ Among the Doctors*

Albrecht Dürer, *Christ Among the Doctors*

William Holman Hunt, *The Finding of the Saviour in the Temple*

above: Gregorio Preti, *Christ Disputing with the Doctors*

opposite: Jean Le Clerc, *Christ Among the Doctors*

Marco D'Oggiono, *The Saviour*

Guido Reni, *Christ Embracing St. John the Baptist*

And Jesus increased in wisdom and stature, and in favour with God and man.

– LUKE 2:52

HIS MINISTRY

And it came to pass in those days, that Jesus came from Nazareth of Galilee, and was baptized of John in Jordan. And straightway coming up out of the water, he saw the heavens opened, and the Spirit like a dove descending upon him: And there came a voice from heaven, saying, Thou art my beloved Son, in whom I am well pleased.

— MARK 1:9–11

Giotto di Bondone, *The Baptism of Christ*

Titian (Tiziano Vecelli), *The Baptism of Christ*

Hendrick Krock, *The Baptism of Christ*

Calisto Piazza, *The Baptism of Christ*

Pietro Perugino, *The Baptism of Christ* (fresco)

*And Jesus returned in the power of the Spirit into Galilee: and there went out
a fame of him through all the region round about.* — LUKE 4:14

And he was there in the wilderness forty days, tempted of Satan; and was with the wild beasts; and the angels ministered unto him.

— MARK 1:13

Get thee behind me, Satan: for it is written, Thou shalt worship the Lord thy God, and him only shalt thou serve.

— LUKE 4:8

Titian (Tiziano Vecelli), *The Temptation of Christ*

Raphael, *The Miraculous Draught of the Fishes* (tapestry)

Follow me, and I will make you fishers of men. – MATTHEW 4:19

Duccio di Buoninsegna, *The Calling of the Apostles Peter and Andrew*

And Jesus went about all Galilee, teaching in their synagogues, and preaching the gospel of the kingdom, and healing all manner of sickness and all manner of disease among the people.

– MATTHEW 5:23

above: Antonella da Messina, *Christ Blessing*

opposite: Giampietrino/Giovan Pietro Rizzoli, *Christ The Redeemer*

47

And seeing the multitudes, he went up into a mountain: and when he was set, his disciples came unto him: And he opened his mouth, and taught them, saying,

Blessed are the poor in spirit: for theirs is the kingdom of heaven.

Blessed are they that mourn: for they shall be comforted.

Blessed are the meek: for they shall inherit the earth.

Blessed are they which do hunger and thirst after righteousness: for they shall be filled.

Blessed are the merciful: for they shall obtain mercy.

Blessed are the pure in heart: for they shall see God.

Blessed are the peacemakers: for they shall be called the children of God.

Blessed are they which are persecuted for righteousness' sake: for theirs is the kingdom of heaven.

Blessed are ye, when men shall revile you, and persecute you, and shall say all manner of evil against you falsely, for my sake.

Rejoice, and be exceedingly glad: for great is your reward in heaven: for so persecuted they the prophets which were before you.

– MATTHEW 5:1–12

Titian (Tiziano Vecelli), *Head of Christ*

above: El Greco (Domenikos Theotokópoulos), *The Miracle of Christ Healing the Blind*

Verily, verily I say unto you, The hour is coming, and now is, when the dead shall hear the voice of the Son of God: and they that hear shall live. — JOHN 5:25

For judgment I am come into this world, that they which see not might see; and that they which see might be made blind. — JOHN 9:39

opposite: Bartolomé Estebán Murillo, *Christ Healing the Paralytic at the Pool of Bethesda*

Gerard David, *Christ Taking Leave of His Mother*

Raphael, *The Transfiguration*

And after six days Jesus taketh Peter, James, and John his brother, and bringeth them up into an high mountain apart, and was transfigured before them: and his face did shine as the sun, and his raiment was white as the light.

— MATTHEW 17:1–2

Verily I say unto you, Except ye be converted, and become as little children, ye shall not enter into the kingdom of heaven. Whosoever therefore shall humble himself as this little child, the same is greatest in the kingdom of heaven. And whoso shall receive one such little child in my name receiveth me.

– MATTHEW 18:3–5

Nicolaes Maes, *Christ Blessing the Children*

above: Jusepe de Ribera, *The Saviour*

Suffer little children, and forbid them not, to come unto me: for of such is the kingdom of heaven. — MATTHEW 19:14

opposite: Pacecco de Rosa, *Christ Blessing the Children*

It is written, My house shall be called the house of prayer: but ye have made it a den of thieves.

– MATTHEW 21:13

El Greco (Domenikos Theotokópoulos), *Christ Driving the Money Changers from the Temple*

Peter Paul Rubens, *Christ and the Mary Magdalene Penitent*

Jacopo Robusti/Tintoretto, *Christ in the Home of Mary and Martha*

Lorenzo Lotto, *Christ and the Adulteress*

I am the light of the world: he that followeth me shall not walk in darkness, but shall have the light of life. — JOHN 8:12

Lucas Cranach (the Elder), *Christ and the Adulteress*

above: Masaccio, *The Tribute Money*

Render therefore unto Caesar the things which are Caesar's; and unto God the things that are God's. —MATTHEW 22:21

opposite: Titian (Tiziano Vecelli), *The Tribute Money*

Ryn van Rembrandt (attributed to), *Head of Christ*

I am the good shepherd, and know my sheep, and am known of mine. As the Father knoweth me, even so know I the Father: and I lay down my life for the sheep.

– JOHN 10:14–15

HIS SUFFERING

And as they did eat, Jesus took bread, and blessed, and brake it, and gave to them, and said, Take, eat: this is my body. And he took the cup, and when he had given thanks, he gave it to them: and they all drank of it. And he said unto them, This is my blood of the new testament, which is shed for many.

– MARK 14:22–24

Salvador Dali, *The Sacrament of the Last Supper*

Benvenuto di Giovanni, *The Agony in the Garden*

Father, if thou be willing, remove this cup from me: nevertheless not my will, but thine, be done.   – LUKE 22:42

Hieronymus Bosch (attributed to), *Christ Before Pilate*

And when they had bound him, they led him away, and delivered him to Pontius Pilate the governor. — MATTHEW 27:2

above: Bacchiacca/Francesco Ubertini Verdi, *The Flagellation of Christ*

Then Pilate therefore took Jesus, and scourged him. – JOHN 19:1

opposite: Diego Rodrigues de Silva y Velázquez, *Christ After the Flagellation Contemplated by the Christian Soul*

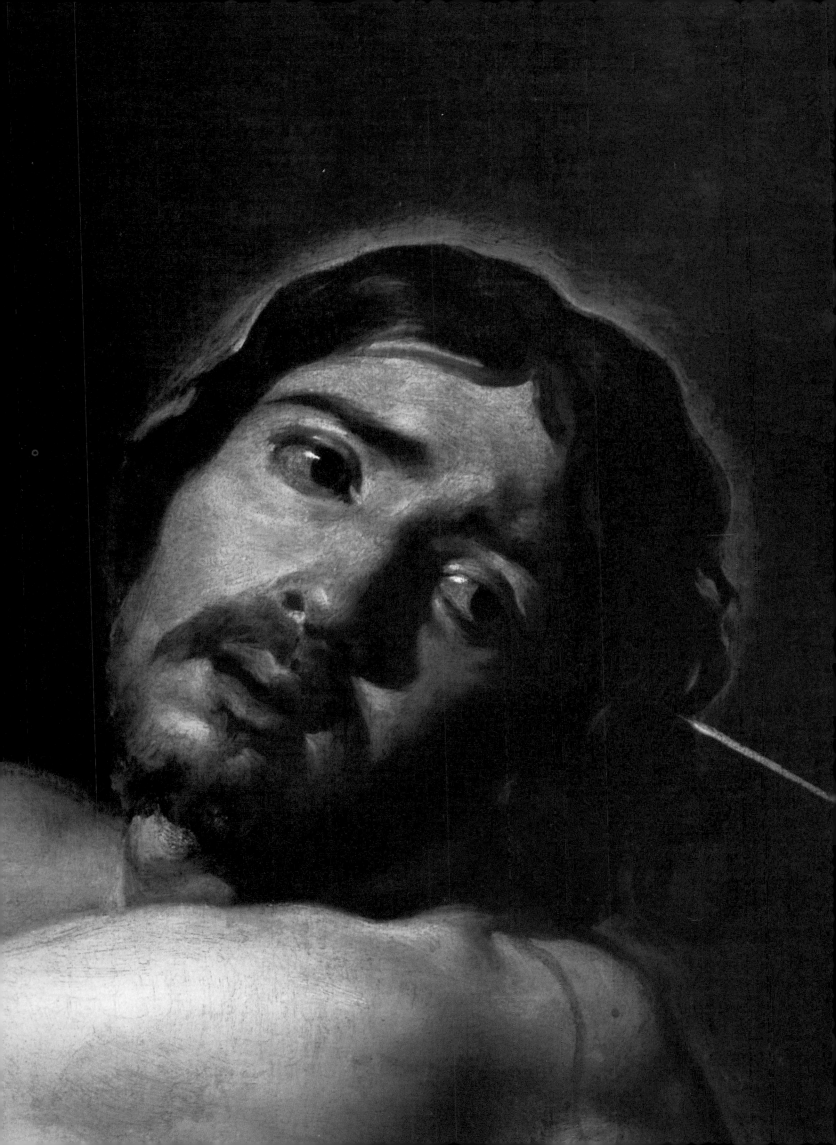

above: Paolo Veronese, *Christ Carrying the Cross*

And the soldiers platted a crown of thorns, and put it on his head, and they put on him a purple robe, and said, Hail, King of the Jews!

— JOHN 19:2–3

opposite: Luis de Morales (El Divino), *Man of Sorrows*

above: Jacopo Robusti/Tintoretto, *Ecce Homo*

opposite: Michelangelo Merisi da Caravaggio, *Ecce Homo*

And they smote him on the head with a reed, and did spit upon him, and bowing their knees worshipped him. And when they had mocked him, they took off the purple from him, and put his own clothes on him, and led him out to crucify him.

– MARK 15:19–20

Sir Anthony van Dyck, *The Mocking of Christ*

And there followed him a great company of people, and of women, which also bewailed and lamented him.

– LUKE 23:27

Gian-Francesco de' Mainieri, *Christ Carrying the Cross*

Andrea Solario, *Christ Carrying the Cross*

Marco Palmezzano, *Jesus Carrying the Cross*

Alessandro Allori, *Simon of Cirene Helping Jesus to Carry the Cross*

above: Domenico Fetti, *The Veil of Veronica*

opposite: Georges Rouault, *Ecce Homo*

And they crucified him, and parted his garments, casting lots: that it might be fulfilled which was spoken by the prophet, They parted my garments among them, and upon my vesture did they cast lots.

— MATTHEW 27:35

Gerard David, *The Crucifixion*

Now from the sixth hour there was darkness over all the land unto the ninth hour.

– MATTHEW 27:45

And when Jesus had cried with a loud voice, he said, Father, into thy hands I commend my spirit: and having said thus, he gave up the ghost.

– LUKE 23:46

Pesellino/Francesco di Stefano, *The Crucifixion with St. Jerome and St. Francis*

Fra Angelico, *Deposition of Christ*

Master of the Avignon School, *Pietà*

And, behold, the veil of the temple was rent in twain from the top to the bottom; and the earth did quake, and the rocks rent; And the graves were opened; and many bodies of the saints which slept arose, and came out of the graves after his resurrection, and went into the holy city, and appeared unto many.

– MATTHEW 27:51–53

Carlo Crivelli, *Pietà*

above: Guercino/Giovanni Francesco Barbieri, *The Dead Christ Mourned by Two Angels*

opposite: Filippino Lippi, *Pietà*

When the even was come, there came a rich man of Arimathaea, named Joseph, who also himself was Jesus' disciple: He went to Pilate, and begged the body of Jesus. Then Pilate commanded the body to be delivered. And when Joseph had taken the body, he wrapped it in a clean linen cloth, and laid it in his own new tomb, which he had hewn out in the rock: and he rolled a great stone to the door of the sepulchre, and departed.

— MATTHEW 27:57–60

Andrea Solario, *Lamentation*

HIS TRIUMPH

In the end of the sabbath, as it began to dawn toward the first day of the week, came Mary Magdalene and the other Mary to see the sepulchre. And, behold, there was a great earthquake: for the angel of the Lord descended from heaven, and came and rolled back the stone from the door, and sat upon it. His countenance was like lightning, and his raiment white as snow: And for fear of him the keepers did shake, and became as dead men. And the angel answered and said unto the women, Fear not ye: for I know that ye seek Jesus, which was crucified. He is not here: for he is risen, as he said.

— MATTHEW 28:1–6

Piero della Francesca, *The Resurrection of Christ*

above: Gaudenzio Ferrari, *Christ Rising from the Tomb*

opposite: Ambrogio Bergognone/Ambrogio di Stefano Borgognone, *The Resurrection*

Now when Jesus was risen early the first day of the week, he appeared first to Mary Magdalene, out of whom he had cast seven devils.

– MARK 16:9

Touch me not; for I am not yet ascended to my Father: but go to my brethren, and say unto them, I ascend unto my Father, and your Father; and to my God, and your God.

– JOHN 20:17

Andrea Orcagna, *Noli me Tangere* (pinnacle from an altarpiece)

Then the same day at evening, being the first day of the week, when the doors were shut where the disciples were assembled for fear of the Jews, came Jesus and stood in the midst, and saith unto them, Peace be unto you.

– JOHN 20:19

Michelangelo Merisi da Caravaggio, *The Supper at Emmaus*

Then said Jesus to them again, Peace be unto you: as my Father hath sent me, even so send I you. And when he had said this, he breathed on them, and saith unto them, Receive ye the Holy Ghost: Whose soever sins ye remit, they are remitted unto them; and whose soever sins ye retain, they are retained.

– JOHN 20:21–23

Diego Rodrigues de Silva y Velázquez, *The Supper at Emmaus*

Cimabue (follower of), *Christ between St. Peter and St. James Major*

Tomasso di Niccolo (attributed to), *Head of Christ*

Giovanni Battista Cima da Conegliano, *The Doubting of St. Thomas*

*Thomas, because thou hast seen me, thou hast believed: blessed are they that have not seen,
and yet have believed.*   – JOHN 20:29

Albrecht Dürer, *Salvator Mundi*

above: The Lombard School, *Christ Blessing*

opposite: Jan van Scorel, *The Benediction of Christ*

Joos van Cleve, *Christ Blessing*

Jan Gossae-t/Mabuse, *Between the Virgin and St. John the Baptist*

117

All power is given unto me in heaven and in earth. Go ye therefore, and teach all nations, baptizing them in the name of the Father, and of the Son, and of the Holy Ghost: Teaching them to observe all things whatsoever I have commanded you: and, lo, I am with you always, even unto the end of the world. Amen.

– MATTHEW 28:18–20

And he led them out as far as to Bethany, and he lifted up his hands, and blessed them. And it came to pass, while he blessed them, he was parted from them, and carried up into heaven.

– LUKE 24:50–51

Sir Anthony van Dyck, *Christ*

Byzantine mosaic (12th century), *Christ Pantocrator*

Artist of the Kremlin, *Icon with the True Image of Christ*

And there shall be signs in the sun, and in the moon, and in the stars; and upon the earth distress of nations, with perplexity; the sea and the waves roaring; Men's hearts failing them for fear, and for looking after those things which are coming on the earth: for the powers of heaven shall be shaken. And then shall they see the Son of man coming in a cloud with power and great glory. And when these things begin to come to pass, then look up, and lift up your heads; for your redemption draweth nigh.

— LUKE 21:25–28

Melozzo da Forli, *Christ the Redeemer*

Behold, he cometh with clouds; and every eye shall see him, and they also which pierced him: and all kindreds of the earth shall wail because of him. Even so, Amen. I am Alpha and Omega, the beginning and the ending, saith the Lord, which is, and which was, and which is to come, the Almighty.

– REVELATION 1:7–8

Matthias Grunewald, *Christ Rising* (from The Isenheim Altarpiece)

LIST OF COLOR PLATES

Note: All the reproductions in this book are details.

Frontispiece:
Bernardino Luini, Italian (Milanese),
1480-1532
Bust of Christ
Courtesy of the Metropolitan Museum of Art, New
York

9. Georges de La Tour, French,
1593-1652
The Newborn Child (Nativity)
Musée des Beaux-Arts, Rennes
Courtesy of Giraudon/Art Resource, New York

10. Raphael, Italian (Umbrian),
1483-1520
Madonna of the Grand Duke
Galleria Palatina, Pitti Palace, Florence
Courtesy of Scala/Art Resource, New York

11. Giovanni Bellini, Italian (Venetian),
1430-1516
Madonna degli Alberelli
Accademia, Venice
Courtesy of Scala/Art Resource, New York

12. Neroccio de' Landi, Italian (Sienese),
1447-1500
*Madonna and Child with St. Anthony Abbot
and St. Sigismund*
Courtesy of the National Gallery of Art, Washington
Samuel H. Kress Collection

13. The School of Piero della Francesca, Italian
(Umbrian),
1410/20-1492
Virgin and Child with Angels
Cambo Collection, Barcelona
Courtesy of Stockphotos, Inc., New York

14. Domenico Ghirlandaio, Italian (Florentine),
1449-1494
Madonna and Child
Courtesy of the National Gallery of Art, Washington
Samuel H. Kress Collection

15. Lucas Cranach (the Elder), German,
1472-1553
Madonna and Child
Courtesy of the National Gallery of Art, Washington
Gift of Adolph Casper Miller

16. Raphael, Italian (Umbrian),
1483-1520
The Alba Madonna
Courtesy of the National Gallery of Art, Washington
Andrew W. Mellon Collection

17. Giovanni Battista Tiepolo, Italian (Venetian),
1691-1770
Madonna of the Goldfinch
Courtesy of the National Gallery of Art, Washington
Samuel H. Kress Collection

18. Ludovico Carracci, Italian (Bolognese),
1555-1619
The Dream of St. Catherine of Alexandria
Courtesy of the National Gallery of Art, Washington
Samuel H. Kress Collection

19. Michelangelo Merisi da Caravaggio, Italian,
1571-1610
Madonna dei Palafrenieri
Galleria Borghese, Rome
Courtesy of Scala/Art Resource, New York

20. Jacopo da Pontormo, Italian (Florentine),
1494-1556/7
The Holy Family
Courtesy of the National Gallery of Art, Washington
Samuel H. Kress Collection

21. Jacob Jordaens, Flemish,
1593-1678
The Holy Family and St. John the Baptist
Courtesy of the Trustees, The National Gallery,
London

22 Byzantine, 13th Century
Madonna and Child on a Curved Throne
Courtesy of the National Gallery of Art, Washington
Andrew W. Mellon Collection

23. Margaritone d'Arezzo, Italian (Tuscan),
active the second half of the 13th Century
Madonna and Child Enthroned
Courtesy of the National Gallery of Art, Washington
Samuel H. Kress Collection

25. Georges de La Tour, French,
1593-1652
St. Joseph the Carpenter
The Louvre, Paris
Courtesy of Giraudon/Art Resource, New York

26. Master of the Catholic Kings, Castilian,
late 15th Century
Christ Among the Doctors
Courtesy of the National Gallery of Art, Washington
Samuel H. Kress Collection

28. Albrecht Dürer, German,
1471-1528
Christ Among the Doctors
Thyssen Collection, Madrid
Courtesy of Scala/Art Resource, New York

29. William Holman Hunt, British,
1827-1910
The Finding of the Saviour in the Temple
City Museum and Art Gallery, Birmingham
Courtesy of Stockphotos, Inc., New York

30. Gregorio Preti, Italian,
1603-1672
Christ Disputing with the Doctors
Courtesy of the Trustees, The National Gallery,
London.

31. Jean Le Clerc, French,
c. 1585-1633
Christ Among the Doctors
Museo Capitolino, Rome
Courtesy of Stockphotos, Inc., New York

32. Marco D'Oggiono, Italian,
1470-1530
The Saviour
Galleria Borghese, Rome
Courtesy of Stockphotos, Inc., New York

33. Guido Reni, Italian, (Bolognese),
1575-1642
Christ Embracing St. John the Baptist
Courtesy of the Trustees, The National Gallery,
London.

34. The Lombard School, Italian,
16th Century
Jesus Disputing the Doctors in the Temple
Galleria Spada, Rome
Courtesy of Stockphotos, Inc., New York

37. Giotto di Bondone, Italian (Florentine),
1266-1336
The Baptism of Christ
Scrovegni Chapel, Padua
Courtesy of Scala/Art Resource, New York

38. Titian (Tiziano Vecelli), Italian (Venetian),
1490-1576
The Baptism of Christ
Pinacoteca Capitolino, Rome
Courtesy of Stockphotos, Inc., New York

39. Hendrick Krock, Danish,
1671-1738
The Baptism of Christ
Friedriksburg Church, Copenhagen
Courtesy of Stockphotos, Inc., New York

40. Calisto Piazza, Italian (Lombard),
before 1505-1551
The Baptism of Christ
Pinacoteca di Brera, Milan
Courtesy of Stockphotos, Inc., New York

41. Pietro Perugino, Italian,
1448-1523
The Baptism of Christ (fresco)
Sistine Chapel, The Vatican, Rome
Courtesy of Scala/Art Resource, New York

43. Titian (Tiziano Vecelli), Italian (Venetian),
1490-1576
The Temptation of Christ
Courtesy of The Minneapolis Institute of Arts

44. Raphael, Italian (Umbrian),
1483-1520
The Miraculous Draught of the Fishes (tapestry)
Pinacoteca, The Vatican, Rome
Courtesy of Stockphotos, Inc., New York

45. Duccio di Buoninsegna, Italian (Sienese),
1255-1318
The Calling of the Apostles Peter and Andrew
Courtesy of the National Gallery of Art, Washington
Samuel H. Kress Collection

46. Giampietrino/Giovan Pietro Rizzoli, Italian
(Milanese),
early 16th Century
Christ The Redeemer
Bagatti Valsecchi Museum, Milan
Courtesy of Stockphotos, Inc., New York

47. Antonella da Messina, Italian,
1430-79
Christ Blessing
Courtesy of the Trustees, The National Gallery,
London

48. Titian (Tiziano Vecelli), Italian (Venetian),
1490-1576
Head of Christ
Pitti Palace, Rome
Courtesy of Stockphotos, Inc., New York

50. Bartolomé Esteban Murillo, Spanish
1617-82
Christ Healing the Paralytic at the Pool of Bethesda
Courtesy of the Trustees, The National Gallery,
London

51. El Greco (Domenikos Theotokópoulos), Greek,
1541/48-1614
The Miracle of Christ Healing the Blind
Courtesy of The Metropolitan Museum of Art,
New York
Gift of Mr. and Mrs. Charles Wrightsman, 1978

52. Gerard David, Flemish,
born about 1455, died 1523
Christ Taking Leave of His Mother
Courtesy of The Metropolitan Museum of Art,
New York
Bequest of Benjamin Altman, 1913

53. Raphael, Italian (Umbrian),
1483-1520
The Transfiguration
Pinacoteca Apostolica, The Vatican, Rome
Courtesy of Stockphotos, Inc., New York

55. Nicolaes Maes, Dutch,
1634-93
Christ Blessing the Children
Courtesy of the Trustees, The National Gallery,
London

56. Pacecco de Rosa, Italian (Neapolitan),
c. 1607-1656
Christ Blessing the Children
Courtesy of Stockphotos, Inc., New York

57. Jusepe de Ribera, Spanish,
1591-1562
The Saviour
The Prado, Madrid
Courtesy of Stockphotos, Inc., New York

59. El Greco (Domenikos Theotokópoulos), Greek,
1541/48-1614
Christ Driving the Money Changers from the Temple
Courtesy of The Minneapolis Institute of Arts

60. Peter Paul Rubens, Flemish,
1577-1640
Christ and the Mary Magdalene Penitent
Alte Pinakothek, Munich
Courtesy of Scala/Art Resource, New York

61. Jacopo Robusti/Tintoretto, Italian (Venetian),
1518-94
Christ in the Home of Mary and Martha
Alte Pinakothek, Munich
Courtesy of Stockphotos, Inc., New York

62. Lorenzo Lotto, Italian (Venetian),
c. 1480-1556
Christ and the Adulteress
The Louvre, Paris
Courtesy of Giraudon/Art Resource, New York

63. Lucas Cranach (the Elder), German,
1472-1553
Christ and the Adulteress
Courtesy of The Metropolitan Museum of Art,
New York
The Jack and Belle Linsky Collection, 1982

64. Titian (Tiziano Vecelli), Italian (Venetian),
1490-1576
The Tribute Money
Courtesy of the Trustees, The National Gallery,
London

65. Masaccio, Italian (Florentine),
1401-28
The Tribute Money
Church of Santa Maria del Carmine, Florence
Courtesy of Scala/Art Resource, New York

66. Ryn van Rembrandt (attributed to), Dutch,
1606-1669
Head of Christ
Courtesy of The Metropolitan Museum of Art,
New York
The Dr. and Mrs. Isaac D. Fletcher Collection

69. Salvador Dali, Spanish,
1904-1989
The Sacrament of the Last Supper
Courtesy of the National Gallery of Art, Washington
The Chester Dale Collection

70. Benvenuto di Giovanni, Italian (Sienese),
c. 1436, died before 1517
The Agony in the Garden
Courtesy of the National Gallery of Art, Washington
The Samuel H. Kress Collection

71. Hieronymus Bosch (attributed to), Dutch,
c. 1450-1516
Christ Before Pilate
Courtesy of the Art Museum, Princeton University
Gift of Alan Marquand

72. Bacchiacca/Francesco Ubertini Verdi, Italian
(Florentine),
1494-1557
The Flagellation of Christ
Courtesy of the National Gallery of Art, Washington
The Samuel H. Kress Collection

73. Diego Rodrigues de Silva y Velázquez, Spanish,
1599-1660
Christ After the Flagellation Contemplated by the Christian Soul
Courtesy of the Trustees, The National Gallery,
London

74. Luis de Morales (El Divino), Spanish,
1509(?)-1581
Man of Sorrows
Courtesy of The Minneapolis Institute of Arts

75. Paolo Veronese, Italian (Venetian),
c. 1528-88
Christ Carrying the Cross
The Louvre, Paris
Courtesy of Giraudon/Art Resource, New York

76. Michelangelo Merisi da Caravaggio, Italian,
1571-1610
Ecce Homo
Palazzo Rosso, Genoa
Courtesy of Scala/Art Resource, New York

77. Jacopo Robusti/Tintoretto, Italian (Venetian),
1518-94
Ecce Homo
Scuola Grande di San Rocco, Venice
Courtesy of Scala/Art Resource, New York

79. Sir Anthony van Dyck, Flemish,
1599-1641
The Mocking of Christ
Courtesy of The Art Museum, Princeton University
Gift of the Charles Ulrick and Josephine Bay
Foundation, Inc., through Colonel C. Michael Paul

80. Giorgione (attributed to), Italian,
1477/8-1510
or the School of Giovanni Bellini, Italian,
c. 1430/8-1516
Christ Carrying the Cross
Courtesy of Isabella Stewart Gardner Museum,
Boston/Art Resource, New York

82. Gian-Francesco de' Mainieri, Italian (Lombard),
d. 1504/5
Christ Carrying the Cross
Galleria Doria-Pamphili, Rome
Courtesy of Stockphotos, Inc., New York

83. Andrea Solario, Italian (Milanese),
1495-1524
Christ Carrying the Cross
Courtesy of Stockphotos, Inc., New York

84. Marco Palmezzano, Italian,
c. 1460-1539
Jesus Carrying the Cross
Galleria Spada, Rome
Courtesy of Stockphotos, Inc., New York

85. Alessandro Allori, Italian (Florentine),
1535-1607
Simon of Cirene Helping Jesus to Carry the Cross
Galleria Doria-Pamphili, Rome
Courtesy of Stockphotos, Inc., New York

86. Domenico Fetti, Italian (Roman),
c. 1589-1623
The Veil of Veronica
Courtesy of the National Gallery of Art, Washington
The Samuel H. Kress Collection

87. Georges Rouault, French,
1871-1958
Ecce Homo
Modern Religious Art Collection, The Vatican, Rome
Courtesy of Scala/Art Resource, New York

88. Gerard David, Flemish,
active about 1484, died 1523
The Crucifixion
Courtesy of The Metropolitan Museum of Art,
New York
Rogers Fund, 1909

91. Pesellino/Francesco di Stefano, Italian,
(Florentine),
1422-1457
The Crucifixion with St. Jerome and St. Francis
Courtesy of the National Gallery of Art, Washington
The Samuel H. Kress Collection

92. Fra Angelico, Italian (Florentine),
c. 1387-1455
Deposition of Christ
Museo di San Marco, Florence
Courtesy of Scala/Art Resource, New York

93. Master of the Avignon School, French,
mid-15th Century
Pietà
The Louvre, Paris
Courtesy of Scala/Art Resource, New York

95. Carlo Crivelli, Italian (Venetian),
c. 1430-1495
Pietà
Courtesy of The Philadelphia Museum of Art
John G. Johnson Collection

96. Filippino Lippi, Italian (Florentine),
c. 1457-1504
Pietà
Courtesy of the National Gallery of Art, Washington
The Samuel H. Kress Collection

97. Guercino/Giovanni Francesco Barbieri, Italian
(Bolognese),
1591-1666
The Dead Christ Mourned by Two Angels
Courtesy of the Trustees, The National Gallery,
London

98. Andrea Solario, Italian (Milanese),
active 1495-1524
Lamentation
Courtesy of the National Gallery of Art, Washington
The Samuel H. Kress Collection

101. Piero della Francesca, Italian (Umbrian),
c. 1420-1492
The Resurrection of Christ
Panacoteca Communale, Sansepolcro
Courtesy of Scala/Art Resource, New York

102. Gaudenzio Ferrari, Italian,
c. 1471-1546
Christ Rising from the Tomb
Courtesy of the Trustees, The National Gallery,
London

103. Ambrogio Bergognone/Ambrogio di Stefano
Borgognone, Italian, (Milanese),
c. 1453-1523
The Resurrection
Courtesy of the National Gallery of Art, Washington
The Samuel H. Kress Collection

105. Andrea Orcagna, Italian (Florentine),
c. 1308-68
Noli me Tangere (pinnacle from an altarpiece)
Courtesy of the Trustees, The National Gallery,
London

106. Michelangelo Merisi da Caravaggio, Italian,
1571-1610
The Supper at Emmaus
Courtesy of the Trustees, The National Gallery,
London

109. Diego Rodrigues de Silva y Velàzquez, Spanish,
1599-1660
The Supper at Emmaus
Courtesy of The Metropolitan Museum of Art,
New York,
Bequest of Benjamin Altman, 1913

110. Cimabue (follower of), Italian,
late 13th Century
Christ between St. Peter and St. James Major
Courtesy of the National Gallery of Art, Washington
Andrew W. Mellon Collection

111. Tomasso di Niccolo (attributed to), Italian,
active 1343-76
Head of Christ
Courtesy of The Metropolitan Museum of Art,
New York,
Gift of Jack and Belle Linsky Fund, 1981

112. Giovanni Battista Cima da Conegliano, Italian
(Venetian),
c. 1459-1517
The Doubting of St. Thomas
Accademia, Venice
Courtesy of Scala/Art Resource, New York

113. Albrecht Dürer, German,
1471-1528
Salvator Mundi
Courtesy of The Metropolitan Museum of Art,
New York,

114. The Lombard School, Italian,
early 16th Century
Christ Blessing
Galleria Doria-Pamphili, Rome
Courtesy of Stockphotos, Inc., New York

115. Jan van Scorel, Dutch,
1495-1562
The Benediction of Christ
The Prado, Madrid
Courtesy of Stockphotos, Inc., New York

116. Joos van Cleve, Flemish,
c. 1485-1540
Christ Blessing
The Louvre, Paris
Courtesy of Stockphotos, Inc., New York

117. Jan Gossaert/Mabuse, Flemish,
c. 1478-1532
Between the Virgin and St. John the Baptist
The Prado, Madrid
Courtesy of Stockphotos, Inc., New York

118. Sir Anthony van Dyck, Flemish,
1599-1641
Christ
Stadtische Kunstsammlung, Düsseldorf
Courtesy of Stockphotos, Inc., New York

120. Byzantine mosaic (12th century),
Byzantine (476-1453)
Christ Pantocrator
Duomo Céfalu
Courtesy of Stockphotos, Inc., New York

121. Artist of the Kremlin, Russian,
Armory Workshop, Russian 17th Century
Icon with the True Image of Christ
Courtesy of the Metropolitan Museum of Art,
New York
The Rogers Fund, 1975

122. Melozzo da Forli, Italian (Umbrian),
1438-94
Christ the Redeemer
Galleria Nazionale delle Marche, Urbino
Courtesy of Scala/Art Resource, New York

125. Matthias Grunewald, German,
c. 1475-1528
Christ Rising (from The Isenheim Altarpiece)
Musee Unterlinden, Colmar
Courtesy of Stockphotos, Inc., New York